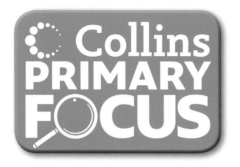

Spelling

Introductory Pupil Book

Joyce Vallar and Carol Doncaster

William Collins' dream of knowledge for all began with the publication of his first book in 1819. A self-educated mill worker, he not only enriched millions of lives, but also founded a flourishing publishing house. Today, staying true to this spirit, Collins books are packed with inspiration, innovation and practical expertise. They place you at the centre of a world of possibility and give you exactly what you need to explore it.

Collins. Freedom to teach.

Published by Collins
An imprint of HarperCollins*Publishers* Ltd.
77–85 Fulham Palace Road
Hammersmith
London
W6 8JB

Browse the complete Collins catalogue at
www.collinseducation.com

Text, design and illustrations © HarperCollins*Publishers* 2011

Previously published as *Collins Focus on Spelling*, first published 2002.

10 9 8 7 6 5 4 3 2 1

ISBN: 978-0-00-742655-3

Joyce Vallar and Carol Doncaster assert their moral right to be identified as the authors of this work.

British Library Cataloguing in Publication Data
A Catalogue record for this publication is available from the British Library.

Cover template: Laing and Carroll
Cover illustration: Q2A Media
Series design: Neil Adams and Garry Lambert
Illustrations: Steve Evans, Kevin Hopgood, Sascha Lipscomb, Lynda Murray, James Walmesley, Gwyneth Williamson

Printed and bound by Printing Express Limited, Hong Kong.

Contents

The alphabet

Did you know that the alphabet is made up of **vowels** and **consonants**?

There are 26 letters in the alphabet.
There are five **vowels**:

a e i o u

The other letters are called **consonants**.
All words have a **vowel** or the letter **y** in them.

Getting started

Write a word to name each picture.
Underline the vowel in each word.

1.

cu̲p

2.

d_____

3.

b_____

4.

b_____

5.

v____

6.

s_____

7.

r_____

8.

f_____

9.

c_____

More to think about

Change the vowel to make new words.

1. hat → _hut_ → _hot_
2. pen → _____ → _____
3. fin → _____ → _____
4. sick → _____ → _____
5. lift → _____ → _____
6. flip → _____ → _____

Now try these

Rhyming helps with spelling.

Change the first consonant to make two more rhyming words each time. The first one has been done to help you.

1. pan → _can_ → _man_
2. run → _____ → _____
3. jet → _____ → _____
4. dog → _____ → _____
5. lip → _____ → _____
6. wag → _____ → _____
7. men → _____ → _____
8. pit → _____ → _____
9. hut → _____ → _____
10. hot → _____ → _____

The long vowel sound *a*

How do you spell words with the long vowel sound *a*, as in *cake*, *rain* and *play*?

The long vowel sound *a* can be spelled in different ways.

a_e as in cake

ai as in rain

ay as in play

Getting started

Write a word to name each picture.
Circle the letters that make the long *a* sound.

1.
c(a)k(e)_____

2.
c_____

3.
w_____

4.
g_____

5.
r_____

6.
c_____

7.
g_____

8.
s_____

9.
p_____

More to think about

1. **Write a word to name each picture.**
   Circle the letters that make the long _a_ sound.

   a)

   r(ai)n _____

   b)

   c_____

   c)

   p_____

   d)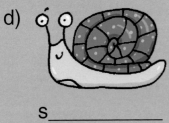

   s_____

   e)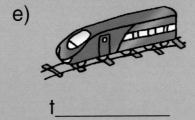

   t_____

   f)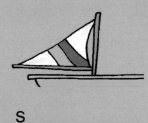

   s_____

2. **Use the clues to work out the _ai_ words.**

   a) a path or marks you can follow ➡ tr_____

   b) drops of hard, icy rain ➡ h_____

   c) what a dog wags ➡ t_____

Now try these

Read this rhyme.

I say, don't stay,
Come away and play.

1. **Write the rhyming words in a list.**

2. **Add more words that end with _-ay_ to your list.**

3. **Write a short rhyme using words from your list.**

The long vowel sound o

How do you spell words with the long vowel sound **o**, as in *coat*, *rose* and *crow*?

The long vowel sound **o** can be spelled in different ways.

oa   as in coat

o_e as in rose

ow   as in crow

Getting started

Write an *oa* word to name each picture.
Circle the letters that make the long *o* sound.

1.

   b(oa)t_____

2.

   f_____

3.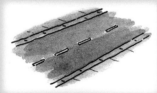

   r_____

4.

   t_____

5.

   s_____

6.

   cl_____

7.

   g_____

8.

   g_____

9.

   c_____

More to think about

Rhyming helps with spelling.

1. Change the first letter to make a rhyming word.
   Circle the letters that make the long *o* sound.
   a) cone → b(o)n(e)
   b) hope
   c) rode

2. Change the first letter to make at least
   three more rhyming words each time.
   The first one has been done to help you.
   a) mole → pole → vole → hole
   b) poke
   c) hose

Now try these

Read this rhyme.

I know that crow in the snow with a bow!

1. a) Write the rhyming words in a list.
   b) Add more *ow* words to your list.
   c) Write a short rhyme using words from your list.

2. Write at least three more words for each different way
   the long *o* sound can be written.

oa	o_e	ow
throat	cone	flow

The long vowel sound e

How do you spell words with the long vowel sound **e**, as in *seat* and *feet*?

The long vowel sound **e** can be spelled in different ways.

ea   as in se**a**t

ee   as in feet

Getting started

Write an *ea* word to name each picture.
Circle the letters that make the long *e* sound.

1.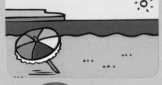

   b(ea)ch _____

2.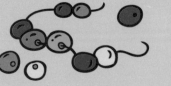

   b_____

3.

   p_____

4.

   s_____

5.

   m_____

6.

   l_____

7.

   t_____

8.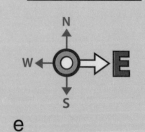

   e_____

9.

   d_____

More to think about

Add letters to make words.

1.
-eep

↓ ↓

<u>sheep</u> _____

2.
-eel

↓ ↓

_____ _____

3.
-eet

↓ ↓

_____ _____

4.
-eed

↓ ↓

_____ _____

5.
-eek

↓ ↓

_____ _____

6.
-ee

↓ ↓

_____ _____

Now try these

Choose the correct words to complete these sentences.

1. Annie likes to splash in the __<u>sea</u>__ .
   (see, sea)

2. I have _____ to London to _____ the queen.
   (been, bean)   (see, sea)

3. There are seven days in a _____.
   (week, weak)

4. Hassan likes to _____ books.
   (reed, read)

5. I went to _____ my friend.
   (meet, meat)

The long vowel sound *u*

How do you spell words with the long vowel sound **u**, as in *moon*, *flew*, *clue* and *tune*?

The long vowel sound **u** can be spelled in different ways.

oo   as in moon

ew   as in flew

ue   as in clue

u_e as in tune

Getting started

Write a word to name each picture.
Circle the letters that make the long *u* sound.

1.

m(oo)n_____

2.

s_____

3.

g_____

4.

b_____

5.

f_____

6.

b_____

More to think about

Write the words from the box with the long *u* sound.
One has been done to help you.

grew

cut   fuss
sun   grew   root
rut   true   tub
shoot   grub   mood
threw   mug   cute
tube   fuse

Now try these

Use the clues to work out the words.

1. a thin, pointed piece of metal used for fixing things together

    s crew

2. something that helps to solve a problem

    cl_____

3. 12 o'clock in the middle of the day

    n_____

4. almost cold

    c_____

5. a solid shape with six square faces all the same size

    c_____

How do you spell words with the long vowel sound *i*, as in *lie*, *night*, *bike* and *cry*?

The long vowel sound *i* can be spelled in different ways.

ie   as in lie

igh as in night

i_e as in bike

y   as in cry

Getting started

Write a word to name each picture.
Circle the letters that make the long *i* sound.

1.

r igh t _____

2.

f_____

3.

f_____

4.

s_____

5.

t_____

6.

k_____

7.

t_____

8.

p_____

9.

n_____

More to think about

Use the clues to work out the words.
Circle the letters that make the long *i* sound.

1. a woman on her wedding day

   b r (i) d (e)

2. nervous about meeting people

   s_____

3. the brightness from the sun, moon, fires or lamps

   l_____

4. your backbone

   s_____

5. a long narrow piece of cloth, worn with a shirt

   t_____

6. a hut with a yard, where pigs are kept

   s_____

Now try these

1. **Rhyming helps with spelling.**
   Change the first sound to make two more
   rhyming words each time.

   a) -ight → <u>night</u> → _____ → _____

   b) -y → <u>sky</u> → _____ → _____

   c) -ide → <u>hide</u> → _____ → _____

2. **Choose one word from each group.**
   Write three sentences, each using a different word.

A. Write the words. They all contain the long vowel sound *a*.

1.

   s_____

2.

   s_____

3.

   p_____

4.

   t_____

5.

   c_____

6.

   p_____

B. Write the words. They all contain the long vowel sound *o*.

1.

   b_____

2.

   g_____

3.

   s_____

4.

   r_____

5.

   s_____

6.

   b_____

C. Write the words. They all contain the long vowel sound *e*.

1.

s_____

2.

l_____

3.

t_____

4.

p_____

5.

l_____

6.

s_____

D. Write the words. They all contain the long vowel sound *i* or *u*.

1.

p_____

2.

p_____

3.

s_____

4.

t_____

5.

f_____

6.

s_____

Did you know that different letters can make the same sound? Let's look at the letters **oo** and **u**.

The letters **oo** and **u** often make the same sound.

crook

bully

Getting started

Write a word to name each picture.

1.

w**oo**d

2.

p_____

3.

l_____

4.

w_____

5.

b_____

6.

b_____

7.

h_____

8.

f_____

9.

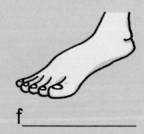

f_____

More to think about

Choose the correct word to complete each sentence.

1. Asam had to __pull__ the sledge up the hill.
   (pull, pool)

2. Tom shouted, "April _____!" when he played the trick.
   (full, fool)

3. I swam to the deep end of the _____.
   (pull, pool)

4. This box is _____ of sweets!
   (full, fool)

Now try these

1. **Add the letters to make words.**

a) l
   t
   br   **-ook**   look
   sh

b) g
   h
   st   **-ood**
   w

2. **Choose one *-ook* word and one *-ood* word. Write a sentence using each one.**

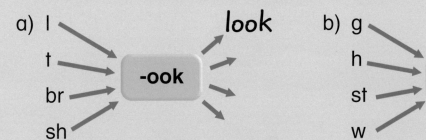
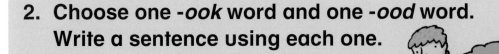

Words with *ar*

How do you spell words with the letter string **ar**, like *car* and *start*?

The sound made by the letters **ar** is the alphabet name **R**.

c**ar**

Getting started

Write a word to name each picture.

1.

p**ark**_____

2.

c_____

3.

s_____

4.

j_____

5.

go-k_____

6.

t_____

7.

c_____

8.

d_____

9.

s_____

More to think about

Add letters to make words.

1.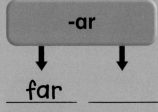

far _____ _____

2.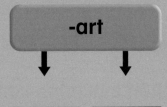

_____ _____

3.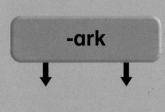

_____ _____

4.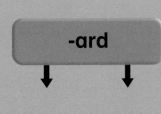

_____ _____

Now try these

Use the clues to work out the words.
Circle the letters that make the *ar* sound in each word.

1. a round pastry case with a fruit filling

t(ar)t_____

2. the third month of the year

M_____

3. a thick covering for a floor, often made of wool

c_____

4. a place where people buy and sell things

m_____

5. land next to a house where people can grow things

g_____

6. the gathering of crops when they are ripe

h_____

Oi **and** *oy*

Did you know that different letters can make the same sound? Let's look at the letters *oi* and *oy*.

The letters *oi* and *oy* often make the same sound.

The letters *oi* are often found in the middle of words.

coin   soil   foil

The letters *oy* are often found at the end of words.

boy   toy   joy

Getting started

1. **Write the words.**

   a) t + oy = __toy__   b) j + oin = _____   c) b + oy = _____

   d) R + oy = _____   e) b + oil = _____   f) s + oil = _____

   g) p + oint = _____   h) j + oy = _____   i) c + oil = _____

2. **Say the words from Question 1.**
   Where do you hear the *oi*/*oy* sound – in the middle or at the end? Write the words in the table.

Middle	End
join	toy

3. **Look at the words in each column. What do you notice?**

More to think about

Write these signs correctly.

1. ★ Joyn the ★ club here

2. Fine top soyl

3. BOIS

4. Boyl in a bag meal
Buy one get one FREE
MEAL FOR TWO

5. Coyns only

6. Tois for sale

Now try these

Find ten *oi* and *oy* words in the wordsearch.
Write each word in the correct column.
Two have been done to help you.

c	o	y	b	j	o	i	n	t	f
g	c	o	i	n	h	j	t	o	y
k	l	p	o	i	n	t	m	p	z
x	s	p	o	i	l	j	o	y	y
r	i	l	b	d	j	o	i	n	p
e	f	b	o	y	s	g	j	n	p
q	w	s	x	z	c	o	i	l	u

oi	oy
joint	coy

Ou and ow

Did you know that different letters can make the same sound? Let's look at the letters **ou** and **ow**.

The letters **ou** and **ow** can make the same sound.

house

cow

Getting started

1. **Write a word to name each picture.**

    a)
    c **lown**

    b)
    c_____

    c)
    _____l

    d)
    c_____

    e)
    f_____

    f)
    b_____

2. **Complete these sentences with *ow* words.**

    a) He drove too fast d_____ the hill.

    b) In autumn, some leaves turn b_____.

More to think about

Add letters to make new words.

1. 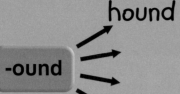 hound

-ound

2. 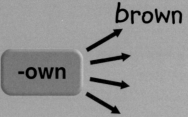 brown

-own

Now try these

1. **Write a word to name each picture.**

a)

c_loud_____

b)

h_____

c)

s_____

2. **Complete these sentences with _ou_ words.**

a) Tom f_ound_ a p_____ coin.

b) A circle is a r_____ shape.

c) Mum will c_____ the money after the sale.

d) She fell on the g_____ and hurt her leg.

e) Mark had to sh_____ for help.

f) The cat chased the m_____.

g) The brass band played l_____ music.

h) The opposite of north is s_____.

Adding -*s*

How do you spell the plural of a noun like *cat*?

For most nouns, just add -**s**.

cat $\longrightarrow$ cat**s**

Getting started

Add -*s* to make each word plural.

1. hat + s = <u>hats</u>
2. mop + s = _____
3. dog + s = _____
4. bun + s = _____
5. hut + s = _____
6. pin + s = _____
7. van + s = _____
8. doll + s = _____
9. lid + s = _____
10. pen + s = _____
11. bed + s = _____
12. net + s = _____
13. bell + s = _____
14. fan + s = _____
15. pram + s = _____
16. frog + s = _____
17. ring + s = _____
18. clock + s = _____
19. shop + s = _____
20. chair + s = _____

More to think about

Write a plural word to name each picture.

1.

t<u>ents</u>

2.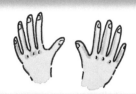

h_____

3.

d_____

4.

c_____

5.

n_____

6.

f_____

7.

p_____

8.

c_____

9.

r_____

Now try these

Copy these sentences.
Make the underlined words plural.

1. Jan jumped in the <u>puddle</u>.

Jan jumped in the puddles.

2. Mandy shut the <u>door</u> to the <u>room</u>.

3. The <u>sweet</u> fell onto the <u>step</u>.

4. I put the <u>book</u> on the <u>table</u>.

5. The <u>boy</u> and <u>girl</u> played with the <u>toy</u>.

Adding *-ed* and *-ing*

What happens when you add **-ed** or **-ing** to a verb like *bark*?

For most verbs, just add **-ed** or **-ing**.

bark ⟶ bark**ed** ⟶ bark**ing**

Getting started

1. Add *-ed* to each word to make a new word.

a) rush → rushed   b) land   c) open

d) play   e) jump   f) push

g) pull   h) want   i) lick

j) moan   k) sail   l) crash

2. Add *-ing* to each word to make a new word.

a) eat → eating   b) lift   c) send

d) lock   e) melt   f) sing

g) kick   h) sell   i) jump

j) bring   k) stand   l) crack

More to think about

Copy and complete the table.

Root word	Add *-ed*	Add *-ing*
lick	licked	licking
look		
sail		
float		
glow		
bang		
rest		
shift		
park		

Now try these

Choose the correct word to complete each sentence.

1. Nick is __pulling__ the rope. (pulling, pulled)

2. He _____ the door of the shed. (locking, locked)

3. Jaz _____ to pack the case. (helped, helping)

4. Wes _____ the ball into the net. (kicked, kicking)

5. Kerry is _____ with a friend. (played, playing)

A. Write a word to name each picture.

1.

c_____

2.

b_____

3.

s_____

4.

s_____

5.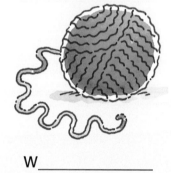

w_____

6.

d_____

B. Write a word to name each picture.

1.

c_____

2.

c_____

3.

b_____

4.

c_____

5.

_____l

6.

m_____

C. Write the singular and plural forms of each word.

1.

    one d_____

    two d_____

2.

    one b_____

    two b_____

3.

    one c_____

    two c_____

4.

    one s_____

    two s_____

5.

    one f_____

    two f_____

6.

    one w_____

    two w_____

D. Copy and complete the table.

Root word	Add *-ed*	Add *-ing*
camp		
land		
melt		
crack		
brush		
bark		
play		
snow		

Or, er, ir, ur, air and ear

What is a letter string?
Let's look at the letter strings **or**, **er**, **ir**, **ur**, **air** and **ear**.

A letter string is a group of letters in a word.

Common letter strings are **or**, **er**, **ir**, **ur**, **air** and **ear**.

Getting started

1. **Use the consonants in the box to make words.**
   You can use the letters more than once.

   | l   c   f   s   st   sn   sh   sw |

   a) <u>l</u>ord   b) __ord   c) __ord

   d) __ort   e) __ort   f) __ort

   g) __ork   h) __ork   i) __ork

2. **Use the consonants in the box to make four more words.**

   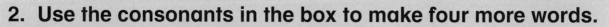
   | c   b   j   h   q   s   t   th |

   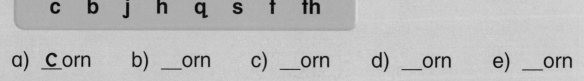
   a) <u>c</u>orn   b) __orn   c) __orn   d) __orn   e) __orn

3. **Which letters were not needed?**

More to think about

The letters **er**, **ir** and **ur** often make a similar sound.

Write a word to name each picture.

1.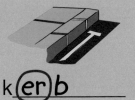

   k(er)b_____

2.

   s_____

3.

   b_____

4.

   n_____

5.

   f_____

6.

   c_____

Now try these

The sound **air** in words can be spelled **ai + r**.
hair

1. **Write only the *air* words from the box.**

chair	chain	fair	hair	stain	stair	pair	pain

The sound **ear** in words can be spelled **ea + r**.
spear

2. **Write only the *ear* words from the box.**

fear	dear	deal	hear	near
heal	clear	spear	clean	shear

Wh, ph and ch

Did you know that two letters can make one sound?

Two letters can spell *one* sound.

w + h ⟶ **wh**eel
p + h ⟶ **ph**otograph

Sometimes **c** + **h** can make the sound **k**.
chorus

Getting started

1. **Write a word to name each picture.**

a)

__wheat__

b)

_____

c)

_____

d)

_____

e)

_____

f)

_____

2. **Use the Look, Say, Cover, Write, Check method to learn to spell these question words.**

| what | where | why | when |

3. **Write one question using each word.**

More to think about

The sound **f** is usually spelled by the letter **f**.

fish

Sometimes the sound **f** is made by the letters **ph**.

phantom

**Complete these words using the letters _ph_
to make the sound _f_.**

1. dolphin
2. al___abet
3. ___otogra___
4. ele___ant
5. tele___one
6. gra___

Now try these

The letters **ch** usually make the sound **ch**.

chicken

The letters **ch** can also make the sound **k** in some words.

chorus

**Use the clues to work out the words
starting with the letters _ch_.**
Hint: you might need to use a
capital letter for one word.

1. a shop where you can buy medicine _____

2. a person in a story _____

3. a Christian festival held on 25 December _____

Compound words

What are compound words? How do you make them?

Compound words are two small words that join to make one word.

wall + paper = wallpaper

Getting started

Join two small words to make one compound word.

1. foot + ball = <u>football</u>
2. black + bird = _____
3. cow + boy = _____
4. down + stairs = _____
5. snow + flake = _____
6. post + box = _____
7. sea + side = _____
8. skate + board = _____
9. tea + pot = _____
10. shoe + lace = _____
11. bed + room = _____
12. rain + bow = _____
13. dust + bin = _____
14. lady + bird = _____

More to think about

Copy and complete the table.

Compound word	Two small words
greenhouse	green + house
postcard	
screwdriver	
seaweed	
sunshine	
homework	
somebody	
cloakroom	
grandmother	
penknife	

Now try these

Which compound words are these?

1.  +  = <u>handbag</u>

2.   +  = _____

3. +  = _____

4.  + = _____

Syllables

What is a syllable? How do you count them?

Each beat in a word is a syllable.

teach/er

syllable 1   syllable 2

com/pu/ter

syllable 1   syllable 2   syllable 3

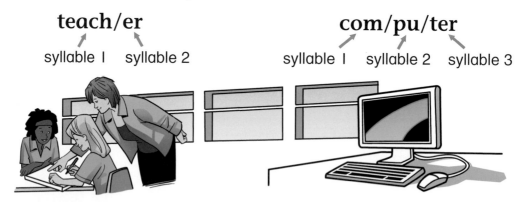

Getting started

Write the words. Mark the syllables.
Write the number of syllables in brackets.

1.

   g<u>ar</u>/<u>den</u> (2)

2.

   p_____c ( )

3.

   e____ph____t ( )

4.

   c_____ ( )

5.

   m_____ ( )

6.

   tele_____ ( )

7.

   r_____ ( )

8.

   pent_____ ( )

9.

   c_____ar ( )

More to think about

One syllable is missing from a word in each sentence.
Add the missing syllables.
Write the sentences correctly.

1. The pan**da** was eating bamboo.
2. Ike and Lucy like to play dom___noes.
3. Houses made from ice are called ig___.
4. The drag___ breathed smoke and flames.
5. There are lots of trees in the gar___.
6. Mr Green was sniffing the flow___.

Now try these

1. Add the missing syllable to complete each month.

   a) Jan/ **u** /ar/y   b) Feb/ru/___ /y   c) _____

   d) Ap/___   e) _____   f) _____

   g) Ju/___   h) Au/_____   i) Sep/___ /ber

   j) Oc/to/___   k) ___ /vem/ber   l) De/___ /ber

2. Copy and complete the table.

Months with one syllable	Months with two syllables	Months with three syllables	Months with four syllables
March			

The prefixes *un-* and *dis-*

What is a prefix? What does it do?
Let's look at the prefixes **un-** and **dis-**.

A prefix is a group of letters at the beginning of a word that can help you work out or change the meaning of the word.

Adding **un-** and **dis-** to words makes the words into their opposites.

un + pack = unpack

dis + obey = disobey

Getting started

1. **Copy these words.**
   Underline the prefix in each one.

   a)

   <u>un</u>zip

   b)

   unlock

   c)

   dislike

   d)

   unhappy

   e)

   disappear

   f)

   disagree

2. **Write the words from Question 1 again.**
   Then write their opposites.
   unzip → zip

More to think about

Add the prefix *un-* to make a new word.

1. un + tidy   = <u>untidy</u>   2. un + load = _____

3. un + even = _____   4. un + true = _____

5. un + dress = _____   6. un + kind = _____

7. un + able = _____   8. un + lucky = _____

9. un + fair = _____   10. un + pack = _____

11. un + like = _____   12. un + safe = _____

Now try these

Choose a word from the box to complete each sentence.

> disobey   dislike   dishonest   disappear   disagree

1. A thief is a **<u>dishonest</u>** person.

2. I _____ fish and chips.

3. If you _____ the rules you will not be in the team.

4. The sun will _____ behind the clouds.

5. Tom and Tina always _____ with each other.

Ow and ea

Did you know that the same letters can make different sounds? Let's look at the letters **ow** and **ea**.

The letters **ow** can make different sounds.

c**ow**   sn**ow**

The letters **ea** can make different sounds.

w**ea**r   h**ea**d   dr**ea**m

Getting started

Add *ow* to complete each word.

1.

cr<u>ow</u>

2.

cl___n

3.

pill___

4.

fl___er

5.

r___

6.

___l

7.

shad___

8.

t___el

9.

m___

More to think about

Add *ea* to complete each word.

1.

p<u>ea</u>r

2.

p___ch

3.

sp___r

4.

s___l

5.

br___d

6.

b___r

7.

b___ds

8.

thr___d

9.

tr___d

Now try these

1. **Read these two sentences aloud.**

   a) The dog has a new <u>lead</u>.

   b) I <u>read</u> my library book last night.

2. **Now use the underlined words in Question 1 to complete these rhymes.**

   a) _____ rhymes with *head*.

   b) _____ rhymes with *bead*.

The suffixes -*ful* and -*ly*

What is a suffix? What does it do?
Let's look at the suffixes -**ful** and -**ly**.

A suffix is added to the end of a word to make a new word.

word		suffix		new word

forget   +   ful   =   forgetful

smooth   +   ly   =   smoothly

Getting started

1. **Add the suffix -*ful* to make a new word.**

   a) help   + ful = <u>helpful</u>

   b) pain   + ful = _____

   c) hand + ful = _____

   d) care   + ful = _____

   e) use   + ful = _____

   f) hope + ful = _____

   g) play   + ful = _____

2. **Choose two words from Question 1.**
   Write a sentence using each one.

More to think about

Add the suffix -*ly* to make a new word.

1. smart + ly = __smartly__

2. lone + ly = _____

3. quick + ly = _____

4. love + ly = _____

5. slow + ly = _____

6. safe + ly = _____

7. calm + ly = _____

8. like + ly = _____

9. loud + ly = _____

10. nice + ly = _____

11. friend + ly = _____

12. sure + ly = _____

Now try these

Choose the correct word to fill each gap.

1. a) The car drove __slowly__ along the street. (slow, slowly)

   b) The car is very _____. (slow, slowly)

2. a) Take good _____ of your bike. (care, careful)

   b) He was _____ when he rode his bike. (care, careful)

3. a) Tariq has a _____ cut on his foot. (pain, painful)

   b) The _____ in my foot is getting better. (pain, painful)

4. a) I hope you have a _____ journey. (safe, safely)

   b) He crossed the road _____. (safe, safely)

45

A. Write a word to name each picture.

1.

f_____

2.

b_____

3.

c_____

4.

c_____

5.

s_____

6.
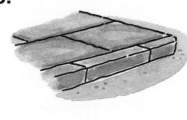
k_____

B. Write a word to name each picture.

1.

d_____

2.
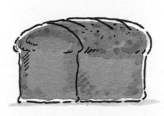
b_____

3.
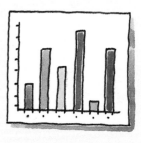
g_____

4.

_____p

5.

_____le

6.

b_____

C. Write the words and mark the syllables.
   Then count the syllables and write the number in brackets.

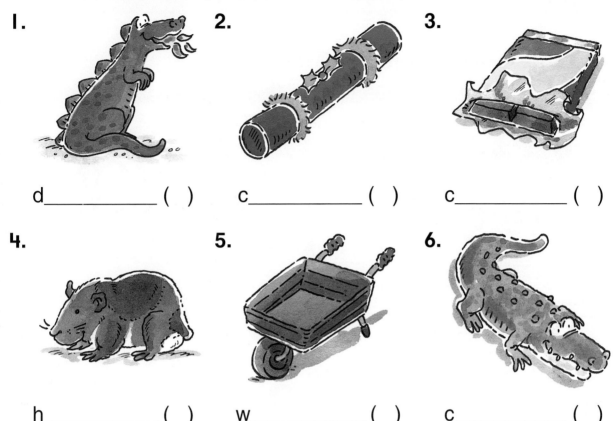

1. d_____ ( )

2. c_____ ( )

3. c_____ ( )

4. h_____ ( )

5. w_____ ( )

6. c_____ ( )

D.

1. Choose the correct prefix to make a new word.

un-	dis-

a) lock   b) obey   c) kind   d) like

e) loyal   f) wind   g) trust   h) lit

2. Choose the correct suffix to make a new word.

-ful	-ly

a) slow   b) care   c) love

d) hope   e) like   f) help

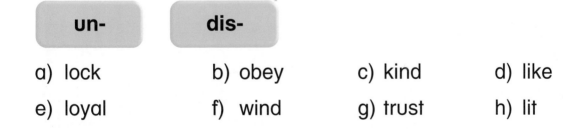

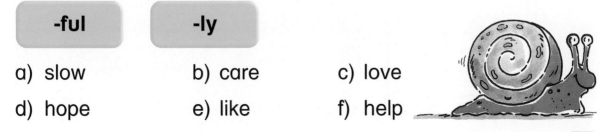

Spellchecker

Write these signs correctly.
Then check the spellings in your dictionary.

1. **Keap off the grass**

2. **Chirch car prk**

3. **Buckets and spaids**

4. **Do not fead the ducks**

6. **Botes for hire**

5. ·Menu·
Roste beef or fish py

7. **M8 Sowth**